Rubber Band Projects

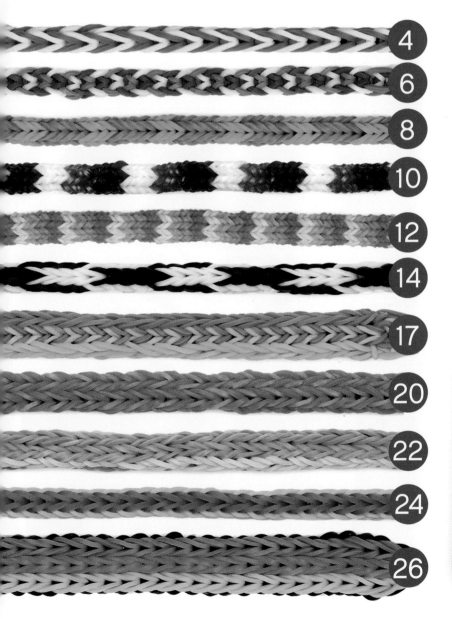

LEISURE ARTS, INC.
Maumelle, Arkansas

Monster Tail® Loom

With the new Monster Tail® loom that fits in your hand, you can take your rubber band jewelry-making everywhere you go! Clear diagrams and easy-to-follow instructions guide you through every step in making 11 great patterns to use for bracelets, necklaces, and rings! You'll love the wide variety of shapes and sizes that are possible, from the single Fishtail to the chunkier Hexafish, Starfish, and Triple Plus. Get ready for never-ending fun!

The Monster Tail Loom is a portable, hand-held loom with a unique arrangement of plastic pins. Bracelets, rings & necklaces in any length are made by placing elastic bands on the loom pins in a pattern & looping them over each other.

Each project has a Chart to show where to place the bands, as well as illustrations to show looping the bands.

Below is a picture of the loom & a blank Chart like the ones used to show band placement. Each ∪ shape represents a loom pin.

The band's color & direction are shown on the Chart & illustrations. It's very important to follow the Steps when placing & looping the bands on the loom pins.

On the illustrations, the band that you are working with is shown in color. Bands that are in the background or not being used for that Step are shown in a much lighter color.

You may find it easier to hold the loom in your hand as you grab & loop the bands. Turn the loom as needed while you work.

Let's get started with a basic Fishtail Bracelet in yellow & purple where you'll learn to place & loop the bands.

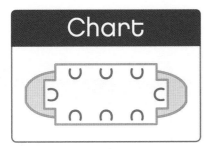

Fishtail Bracelet
Band Placement

• **This bracelet only uses 2 pins.**

Step 1: Use your fingers to twist a yellow band into a figure 8 & place it on the pins. Push it down on the pins.

Step 2: Place a purple band on top the yellow band on the pins. Push it down on the pins.

Step 3: Place a yellow band on top the purple band on the pins. Push it down on the pins.

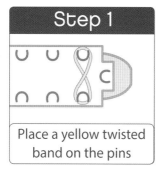
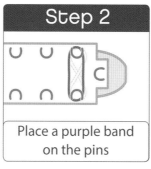
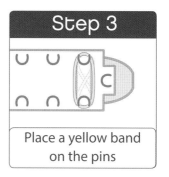

Step 1	Step 2	Step 3
Place a yellow twisted band on the pins	Place a purple band on the pins	Place a yellow band on the pins

Looping

When Looping the Bands:
• **Always use the looping tool to pick up & loop the bands.**

Step 1: Grab the bottom yellow band on the lower pin.

Step 2: Loop the band to the center over the other 2 bands (purple & yellow).

Step 3: Grab the bottom yellow band on the top pin.

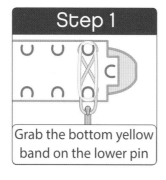
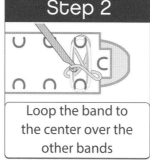
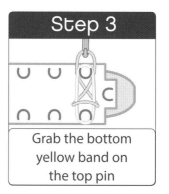

Step 1	Step 2	Step 3
Grab the bottom yellow band on the lower pin	Loop the band to the center over the other bands	Grab the bottom yellow band on the top pin

Step 4: Loop the band to the center over the other 2 bands (purple & yellow).

Step 5: Place a purple band on the pins. Push the bands down.

Step 6: Loop the bottom purple band to the center.

Step 7: Place a yellow band on the pins.

Step 4	Step 5	Step 6	Step 7
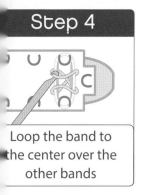	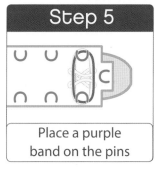	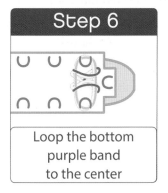	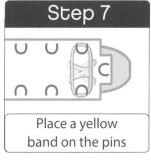
Loop the band to the center over the other bands	Place a purple band on the pins	Loop the bottom purple band to the center	Place a yellow band on the pins

Step 8: Continue looping the bottom band to the center & placing a new band on the pins (alternating the colors). The bracelet will extend from the loom bottom.

Step 9: When the bracelet is long enough, loop the bottom band to the center over the other bands, leaving 1 band on each pin.

Step 10: Grab the last band from the pins & slide it on the looping tool.

Step 11: Slide a C-clip on the band loops at the beginning & end to join.

Step 9	Step 10	Step 11
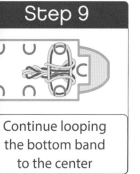	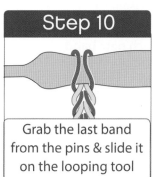	
Continue looping the bottom band to the center	Grab the last band from the pins & slide it on the looping tool	Slide a C-clip on the band loops at the beginning & end to join

That's all there is to it! So easy & so fun. Practice making the Fishtail in several color combinations or repeating color patterns.

5

Inverted Fishtail Bracelet

The illustrations show the red, white & blue version of this bracelet.
Turn a basic Fishtail inside out just by changing how you loop.

Band Placement

When Placing the Bands:

- This bracelet uses 2 pins.
- Use your fingers to place the bands on the loom.
- Push each band down after you place it on the pins.
- Follow the Steps when placing the bands.

Step 1	Step 2	Step 3
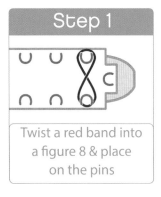	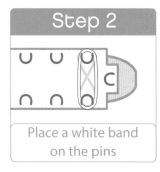	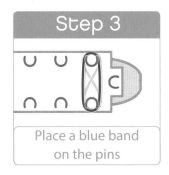
Twist a red band into a figure 8 & place on the pins	Place a white band on the pins	Place a blue band on the pins

Looping

When Looping the Bands:

- Always use the looping tool to pick up & loop the bands.
- Follow the Steps to loop the bands in a consistent order.
- Push the bands down after you place each new band.

Step 1	Step 2	Step 3
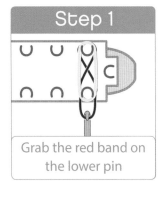	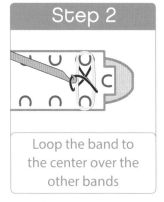	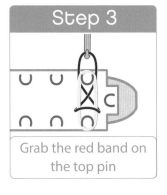
Grab the red band on the lower pin	Loop the band to the center over the other bands	Grab the red band on the top pin

Step 4

Loop the band to the center over the other bands

Step 5
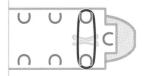
Place a red band on the pins

Step 6a
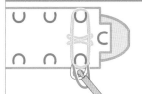
Go behind the middle blue band & grab the white band

Step 6b
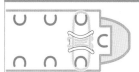
Loop the band to the center

Step 7
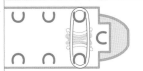
Place a white band on the pins

Step 8

Always going behind the middle band on the pins, continue looping the bottom band to the center

Step 8: Continue looping the bottom band to the center & placing a new band on the pins (following established color order) until the bracelet is the right length.

Step 9: Follow Steps 9-11 of Fishtail Bracelet on page 5 to complete the bracelet.

The matching ring is just a shorter version of the bracelet. Change up the color combos by using red, orange & yellow or brown, white & green.

Trifish Bracelet

The illustrations show the green & pink version of this bracelet.
Using 3 pins gives this bracelet a three-sided shape.

Band Placement

When Placing the Bands:
- This bracelet uses 3 pins.
- Use your fingers to place the bands on the loom.
- Push each band down after you place it on the pins.
- Follow the Steps when placing the bands.

Step 1	Step 2	Step 3
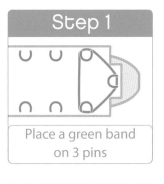	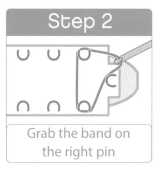	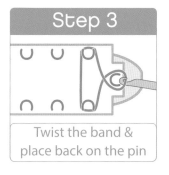
Place a green band on 3 pins	Grab the band on the right pin	Twist the band & place back on the pin

Step 4	Step 5
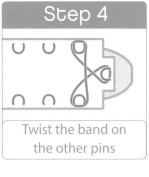	
Twist the band on the other pins	Place 2 more green bands on the pins

To make the more subtle yellow & grey bracelet, use a 4 grey band, 2 yellow band color sequence.

Looping

When Looping the Bands:

- Always use the looping tool to pick up & loop the bands.
- Follow the Steps to loop the bands in a consistent order.
- Push the bands down after you place each new band.

Step 1
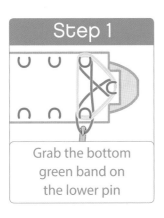
Grab the bottom green band on the lower pin

Step 2
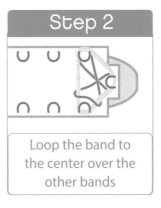
Loop the band to the center over the other bands

Step 3
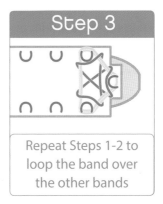
Repeat Steps 1-2 to loop the band over the other bands

Step 4
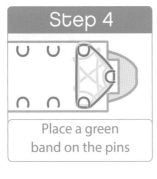
Place a green band on the pins

Step 5
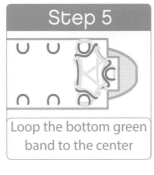
Loop the bottom green band to the center

Step 6

Place a pink band on the pins

Step 7
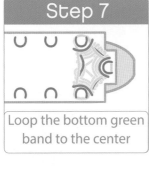
Loop the bottom green band to the center

Step 8: Continue placing a new band on the pins & looping the bottom band to the center (4 pink, 4 green color sequence).

Step 9: When the bracelet is long enough, loop the bottom bands to the center over the other bands, leaving 1 band on each pin.

Step 10
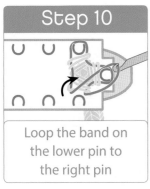
Loop the band on the lower pin to the right pin

Step 11
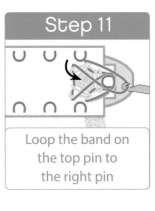
Loop the band on the top pin to the right pin

Step 12

Grab the bands on the right pin & slide them on the hook

Step 13

Slide a C-clip on the band loops at the beginning & end to join

Quadfish Bracelet

The illustrations show the violet, navy & white version of this bracelet.

Using 4 pins gives this bracelet a square shape that is very pretty when made into a necklace & ring.

Band Placement

When Placing the Bands:

- This bracelet uses 4 pins.
- Use your fingers to place the bands on the loom.
- Push each band down after you place it on the pins.
- Follow the Steps when placing the bands.

Step 1

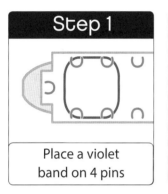

Place a violet band on 4 pins

Step 2

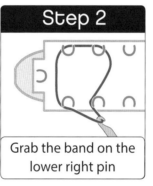

Grab the band on the lower right pin

Step 3

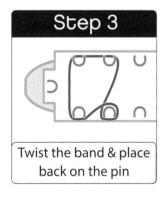

Twist the band & place back on the pin

Step 4

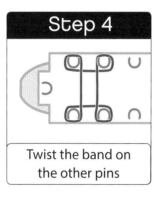

Twist the band on the other pins

Step 5

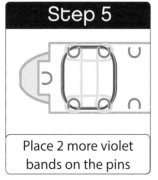

Place 2 more violet bands on the pins

It's easy to make a necklace or ring. Just keep adding bands until the necklace will slip over your head & not be tight on your neck. The ring is simply a short bracelet. For the grey & aqua set, alternate 12 grey bands with 4 aqua bands.

Looping

When Looping the Bands:

- Always use the looping tool to pick up & loop the bands.
- Follow the Steps to loop the bands in a consistent order.
- Push the bands down after you place each new band.

Step 1
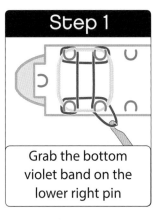
Grab the bottom violet band on the lower right pin

Step 2
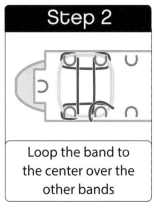
Loop the band to the center over the other bands

Step 3
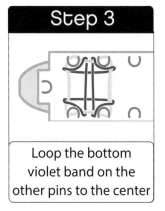
Loop the bottom violet band on the other pins to the center

Step 4
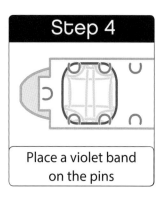
Place a violet band on the pins

Step 5
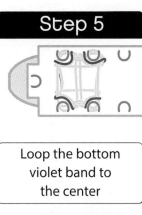
Loop the bottom violet band to the center

Step 6
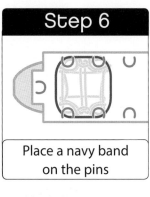
Place a navy band on the pins

Step 7: Continue looping the bottom band to the center & placing 1 new band on the pins (4 violet, 4 navy, 4 white color sequence).

Step 8: When the bracelet is long enough, loop the bottom band on each pin to the center over the other bands, leaving 1 band on each pin.

Step 9
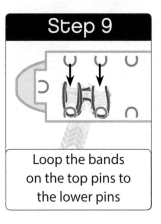
Loop the bands on the top pins to the lower pins

Step 10
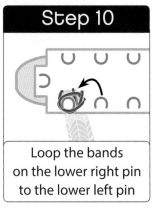
Loop the bands on the lower right pin to the lower left pin

Step 11

Grab the bands & slide them on the hook

Step 12
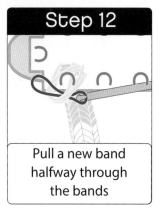
Pull a new band halfway through the bands

Step 13
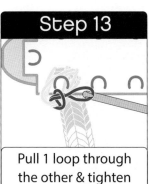
Pull 1 loop through the other & tighten

Step 14: Carefully remove the bands from the pin. Slide a C-clip on the band loops at the beginning & end to join.

11

Hexafish Bracelet

The illustrations show the neon rainbow version of this bracelet.
Using 6 pins gives this bracelet a very round shape.

Band Placement

When Placing the Bands:

- This bracelet uses 6 pins.
- Use your fingers to place the bands on the loom.
- Push each band down after you place it on the pins.
- Follow the Steps when placing the bands.

Step 1

Place an orange band on 6 pins

Step 2

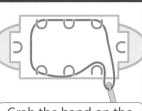

Grab the band on the lower right pin

Step 3

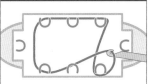

Twist the band & place back on the pin

Step 4

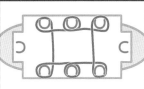

Twist the band on the other pins

Step 5

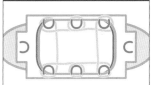

Place an orange & then a green band on the pins

Whether you use hot neon or traditional rainbow colors, this bracelet lets your creativity shine.

Looping

When Looping the Bands:

- Always use the looping tool to pick up & loop the bands.
- Follow the Steps to loop the bands in a consistent order.
- Push the bands down after you place each new band.

Step 1
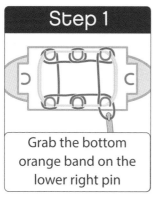
Grab the bottom orange band on the lower right pin

Step 2
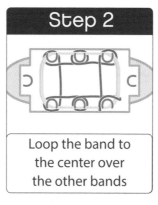
Loop the band to the center over the other bands

Step 3
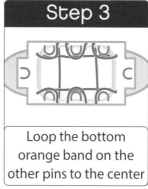
Loop the bottom orange band on the other pins to the center

Step 4
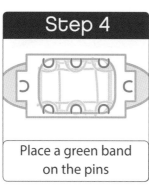
Place a green band on the pins

Step 5
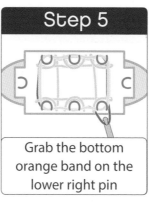
Grab the bottom orange band on the lower right pin

Step 6
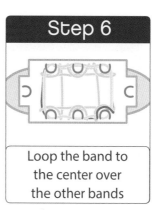
Loop the band to the center over the other bands

Step 7
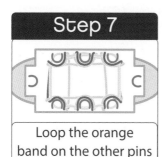
Loop the orange band on the other pins to the center

Step 8: Continue placing a new band on the pins & looping the bottom band to the center (referring to the photo for the color sequence).

Step 9: When the bracelet is long enough, loop the bottom band on each pin to the center over the other bands, leaving 1 band on each pin.

Step 10
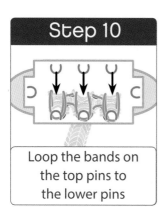
Loop the bands on the top pins to the lower pins

Step 11
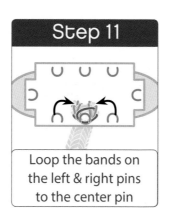
Loop the bands on the left & right pins to the center pin

Step 12: Follow Steps 11-14 of Quadfish Bracelet on page 11 to complete the bracelet.

Double X's Bracelet

The illustrations show the black & white checkerboard version of this bracelet.

Using 4 pins gives this bracelet a square shape that also looks great in alternating green & blue bands (shown on page 16).

Band Placement

When Placing the Bands:

- This bracelet uses 4 pins.
- Use your fingers to place the bands on the loom.
- Push each band down after you place it on the pins.
- Follow the Steps when placing the bands.

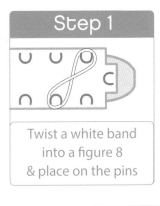

Step 1

Twist a white band into a figure 8 & place on the pins

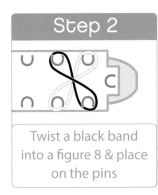

Step 2

Twist a black band into a figure 8 & place on the pins

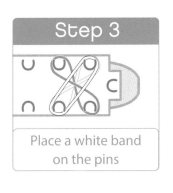

Step 3

Place a white band on the pins

Step 4

Place a black band on the pins

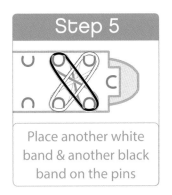

Step 5

Place another white band & another black band on the pins

Looping

When Looping the Bands:
- Always use the looping tool to pick up & loop the bands.
- Follow the Steps to loop the bands in a consistent order.
- Push the bands down after you place each new band.

Step 1
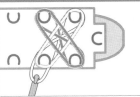
Grab the bottom white band on the lower left pin

Step 2

Loop the band to the center over the other bands

Step 3
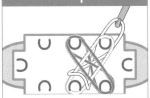
Grab the bottom white band on the top right pin

Step 4

Loop the band to the center over the other bands

Step 5

Loop the bottom black band on the other pins to the center

Step 6

Place a white & a black band on the pins

Step 7

Loop the bottom white & bottom black bands to the center

Step 8

Place a black band over the white bands & a white band over the black bands

Continued on page 16.

15

Step 9

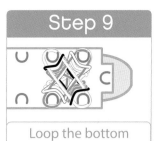

Loop the bottom bands to the center

Step 10: Continue placing new bands on the pins & looping the bottom band to the center, alternating colors after every 4th set of bands.

Step 11: When the bracelet is long enough, loop the bottom band on each pin to the center over the other bands, leaving 1 band on each pin.

Step 12

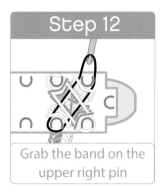

Grab the band on the upper right pin

Step 13

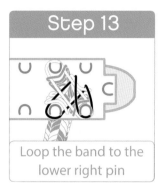

Loop the band to the lower right pin

Step 14

Grab the band on the upper left pin

Step 15

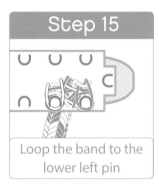

Loop the band to the lower left pin

Step 16

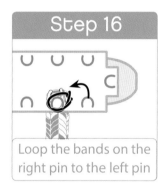

Loop the bands on the right pin to the left pin

Step 17: Follow Steps 11-14 of Quadfish Bracelet on page 11 to complete the bracelet.

Show your school spirit by alternating the team's colors, like we did for the blue & green bracelet.

Interlocking Double X's Bracelet

The illustrations show the green & blue version of this bracelet.
This bracelet has a thick, flat shape that shows off the interlocking colors
of the bands in the middle. Try pink & grey for a fun fashion statement!

Band Placement

When Placing the Bands:
- This bracelet uses 6 pins.
- Use your fingers to place the bands on the loom.
- Push each band down after you place it on the pins.
- Follow the Steps when placing the bands.

Step 1
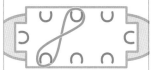
Twist a blue band into a figure 8 & place on the pins

Step 2
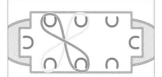
Twist & place the 2nd blue band

Step 3
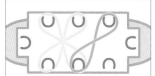
Twist a green band into a figure 8 & place on the pins

Step 4
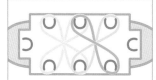
Twist & place the 2nd green band

Step 5
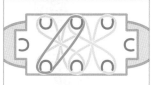
Place the 3rd blue band on the pins

Step 6

Place the 4th blue band on the pins

Step 7

Place the 3rd green band on the pins

Step 8

Place the 4th green band on the pins

Step 9

Place the 5th & 6th blue bands on the pins

Step 10

Place the 5th & 6th green bands on the pins

Continued on page 18.

Looping

When Looping the Bands:

- Always use the looping tool to pick up & loop the bands.
- Follow the Steps to loop the bands in a consistent order.
- Push the bands down after you place each new band.

Step 1

Grab the bottom green band on the lower right pin

Step 2
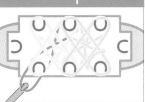
Loop the band to the center over the other bands

Step 3
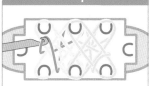
Grab the bottom blue band on the lower left pin

Step 4

Loop the band to the center over the other bands

Step 5

Grab the bottom blue & green bands on the lower center pin

Step 6

Loop the bands to the center over the other bands

Step 7: Repeat Steps 5 & 6, leaving 2 bands (1 blue, 1 green) on the lower pin.

Step 8

Repeat Steps 1-7 on the top row of pins

Step 9

Place 2 blue bands on the pins

Step 10

Loop the bottom blue bands to the center on all 4 pins

Step 11
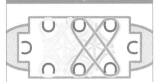
Place 2 green bands on the pins

Step 12

Loop the bottom green bands to the center on all 4 pins

Step 13

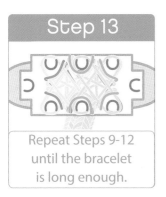

Repeat Steps 9-12 until the bracelet is long enough.

Step 14: Loop the bottom bands on each pin to the center over the other bands, leaving 1 band on each pin.

Step 15

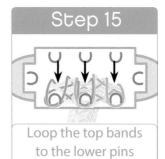

Loop the top bands to the lower pins

Step 16

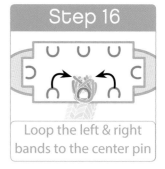

Loop the left & right bands to the center pin

Step 17: Follow Steps 11-14 of Quadfish Bracelet on page 11 to complete the bracelet.

Criss-Cross Bracelet

The illustrations show the blue & pink version of this bracelet.
This bracelet, made on 4 pins, has a bold look when made with highly
contrasting colors & a more natural look when earthy colors are used.

Band Placement

When Placing the Bands:
- This bracelet uses 4 pins.
- Use your fingers to place the bands on the loom.
- Push each band down after you place it on the pins.
- Follow the Steps when placing the bands.

Step 1	Step 2	Step 3	Step 4
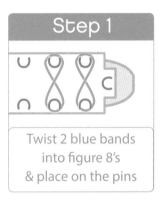		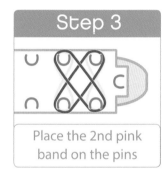	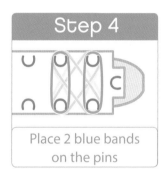
Twist 2 blue bands into figure 8's & place on the pins	Place a pink band on the pins	Place the 2nd pink band on the pins	Place 2 blue bands on the pins

Looping

When Looping the Bands:
- Always use the looping tool to pick up & loop the bands.
- Follow the Steps to loop the bands in a consistent order.
- Push the bands down after you place each new band.

Step 1	Step 2	Step 3	Step 4
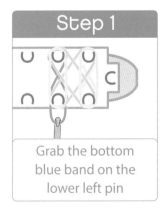	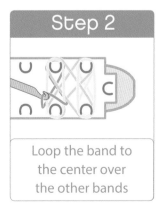	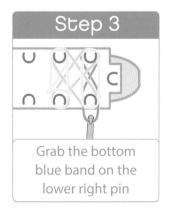	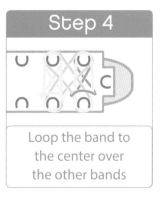
Grab the bottom blue band on the lower left pin	Loop the band to the center over the other bands	Grab the bottom blue band on the lower right pin	Loop the band to the center over the other bands

Step 5
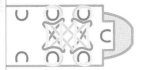
Repeat Steps 1-4 with the bottom blue bands on the top pins

Step 6

Place 2 pink bands on the pins

Step 7
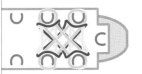
Loop the bottom pink bands to the center over the other bands

Step 8

Place 2 blue bands on the pins

Step 9: Repeat Steps 1-8 until the bracelet is long enough.

Step 10: Loop the bottom band on each pin to the center over the other bands, leaving 1 band on each pin.

Step 11
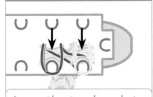
Loop the top bands to the lower pins

Step 12

Loop the right bands to the left pin

Step 13: Follow Steps 11-14 of Quadfish Bracelet on page 11 to complete the bracelet.

This colorful bracelet is great for girls & boys. Alternate green, brown & light brown bands for an earth-tone look.

Starfish Bracelet

Placing the bands in a star shape yields alternating rows of color.

Band Placement

When Placing the Bands:

- This bracelet uses 6 pins.
- Use your fingers to place the bands on the loom.
- Push each band down after you place it on the pins.
- Follow the Steps when placing the bands.

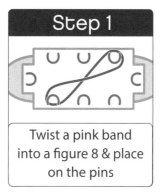

Step 1
Twist a pink band into a figure 8 & place on the pins

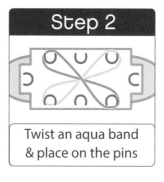

Step 2
Twist an aqua band & place on the pins

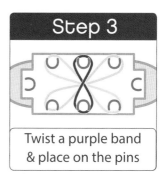

Step 3
Twist a purple band & place on the pins

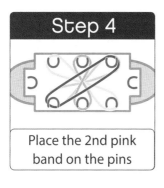

Step 4
Place the 2nd pink band on the pins

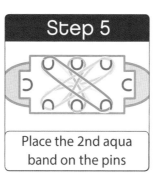

Step 5
Place the 2nd aqua band on the pins

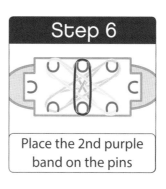

Step 6
Place the 2nd purple band on the pins

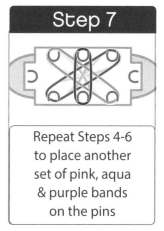

Step 7
Repeat Steps 4-6 to place another set of pink, aqua & purple bands on the pins

Looping

When Looping the Bands:

- Always use the looping tool to pick up & loop the bands.
- Follow the Steps to loop the bands in a consistent order.
- Push the bands down after you place each new band.

Step 1
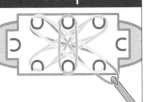
Grab the bottom aqua band on the lower right pin

Step 2
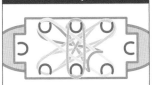
Loop the band to the center over the other bands

Step 3
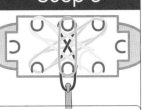
Grab the bottom purple band on the lower center pin

Step 4
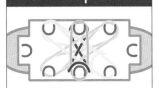
Loop the band to the center over the other bands

Step 5

Grab the bottom pink band on the lower left pin

Step 6

Loop the band to the center over the other bands

Step 7

Repeat Steps 1-6 with the bottom bands on the top pins

Step 8
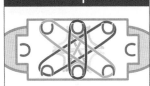
Place a pink band, an aqua band & a purple band on the pins

Step 9: Repeat Steps 1-8 until the bracelet is long enough.

Step 10: Loop the bottom band on each pin to the center over the other bands, leaving 1 band on each pin.

Step 11

Loop the bands on the top pins to the lower pins

Step 12
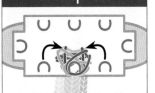
Loop the bands on the left & right pins to the center pin

Step 13: Follow Steps 11-14 of Quadfish Bracelet on page 11 to complete the bracelet.

Single Plus Bracelet

This quick & easy bracelet places the bands in a "+" sign arrangement.

Band Placement

When Placing the Bands:

- This bracelet uses 4 pins.
- Use your fingers to place the bands on the loom.
- Push each band down after you place it on the pins.
- Follow the Steps when placing the bands.

Step 1

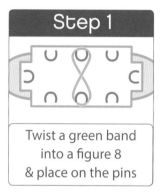

Twist a green band
into a figure 8
& place on the pins

Step 2

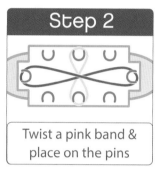

Twist a pink band &
place on the pins

Step 3

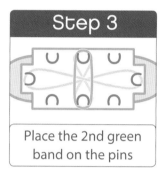

Place the 2nd green
band on the pins

Step 4

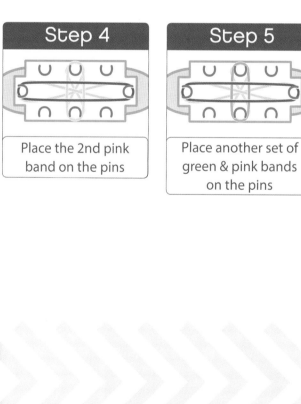

Place the 2nd pink
band on the pins

Step 5

Place another set of
green & pink bands
on the pins

Looping

When Looping the Bands:

• Always use the looping tool to pick up & loop the bands.

• Follow the Steps to loop the bands in a consistent order.

• Push the bands down after you place each new band.

Step 1
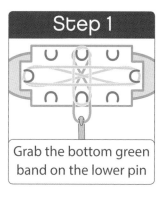
Grab the bottom green band on the lower pin

Step 2
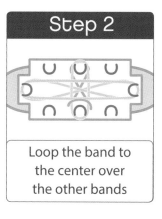
Loop the band to the center over the other bands

Step 3
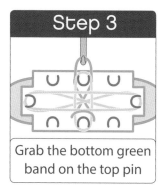
Grab the bottom green band on the top pin

Step 4
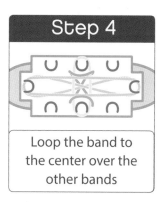
Loop the band to the center over the other bands

Step 5
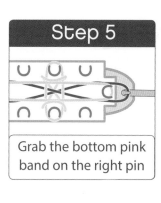
Grab the bottom pink band on the right pin

Step 6
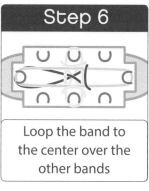
Loop the band to the center over the other bands

Step 7
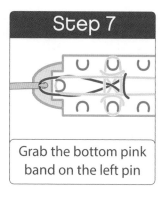
Grab the bottom pink band on the left pin

Step 8
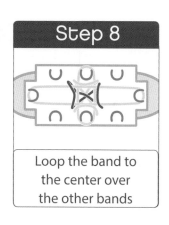
Loop the band to the center over the other bands

Step 9
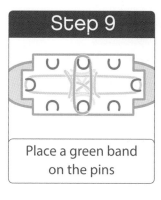
Place a green band on the pins

Step 10
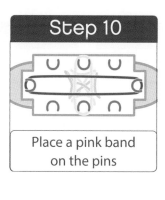
Place a pink band on the pins

Step 11: Repeat Steps 1-10 until the bracelet is long enough.

Step 12: Loop the bottom band on each pin to the center over the other bands, leaving 1 band on each pin.

Step 13
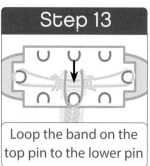
Loop the band on the top pin to the lower pin

Step 14
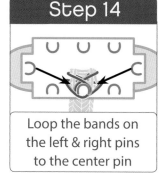
Loop the bands on the left & right pins to the center pin

Step 15: Follow Steps 11-14 of Quadfish Bracelet on page 11 to complete the bracelet.

Triple Plus Bracelet

Using all 8 pins makes a wide 4-color bracelet.

Band Placement

When Placing the Bands:

- This bracelet uses 8 pins.
- Use your fingers to place the bands on the loom.
- Push each band down after you place it on the pins.
- Follow the Steps when placing the bands.

Step 1
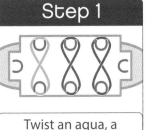
Twist an aqua, a
pink & a purple band
into figure 8's
& place on the pins

Step 2
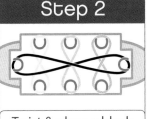
Twist & place a black
band on the pins

Step 3
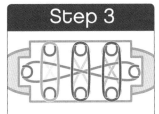
Place the 2nd set of
aqua, pink & purple
bands on the pins

Step 4
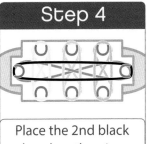
Place the 2nd black
band on the pins

Step 5
Repeat Steps 3-4 to
place the 3rd set of
bands on the pins

Looping

When Looping the Bands:

- Always use the looping tool to pick up & loop the bands.
- Follow the Steps to loop the bands in a consistent order.
- Push the bands down after you place each new band.

Step 1
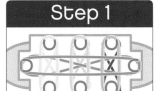
Grab the bottom purple band on the lower right pin

Step 2
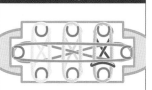
Loop the band to the center over the other bands

Step 3

Grab the bottom pink band on the lower center pin

Step 4
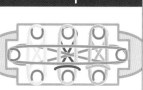
Loop the band to the center over the other bands

Step 5
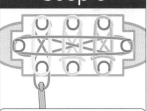
Grab the bottom aqua band on the lower left pin

Step 6
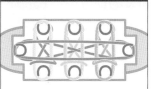
Loop the band to the center over the other bands

Step 7
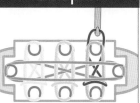
Grab the bottom purple band on the top right pin

Step 8
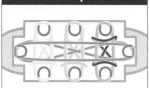
Loop the band to the center over the other bands

Step 9
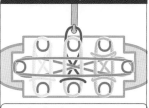
Grab the bottom pink band on the top center pin

Step 10
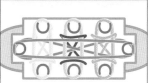
Loop the band to the center over the other bands

Step 11
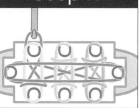
Grab the bottom aqua band on the top left pin

Step 12
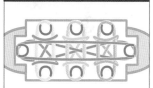
Loop the band to the center over the other bands

Step 13
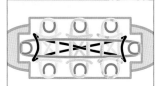
Loop the bottom black band on the left & right pins to the center over the other bands

Step 14
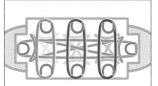
Place aqua, pink, & purple bands on the pins

Step 15
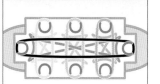
Place a black band on the pins

Continued on page 28.

Step 16: Repeat Steps 1-15 until the bracelet is long enough.

Step 17: Loop the bottom band on each pin to the center over the other bands, leaving 1 band on each pin.

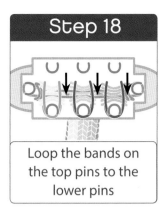

Step 18

Loop the bands on the top pins to the lower pins

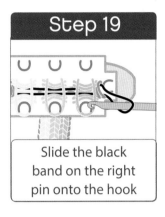

Step 19

Slide the black band on the right pin onto the hook

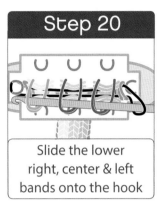

Step 20

Slide the lower right, center & left bands onto the hook

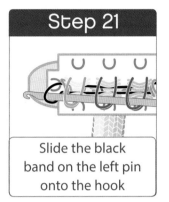

Step 21

Slide the black band on the left pin onto the hook

Step 22: Follow Steps 12-14 of Quadfish Bracelet on page 11 to complete the bracelet.